John Thompson's
Chord-Speller

A Music Writing Book

Including

Major, Minor, Augmented and Diminished Triads

Authentic and Plagal Cadences

Dominant and Diminished Seventh Chords

WILLIS MUSIC

Copyright, MCMXLVII, by The Willis Music Co.
International Copyright Secured
Printed in U. S. A.

Exclusively Distributed By

HAL•LEONARD®
CORPORATION
7777 W. BLUEMOUND RD. P.O. BOX 13819 MILWAUKEE, WI 53213

PREFACE

Intervals

Before studying Chords, pupils should have had preliminary study of Intervals.

A thorough knowledge of Intervals is absolutely essential to an understanding of Chord structure.

John Thompson's SCALE-SPELLER presents Major and Minor Scales as well as Intervals in all forms.

Its use should precede the study of this book.

Review of Major and Minor Thirds

Since all chords are built in Third-steps (major or minor), a review of these intervals is given before Chords are presented.

Writing Book

While this is a Chord-writing book, it is NOT a Harmony Method.   The purpose of the book is to present the Triads (including the Dominant and Diminished Seventh Chords) in a manner that will enable the pupil to read them, write them and recognize them *by sight or sound*.

Only a few of the simplest rules for the movement of voices are given so that the pupil can form the Cadences in all keys.

Dominant and Diminished Seventh Chords

Exercises on the Dominant and Diminished Seventh Chords are restricted to Root Position.

The only resolution required is the progression to the Tonic.

The inversions of these two chords, together with their various resolutions, rightly belong to the study of Harmony and should be taken up at a later period.

Table of Chords

It is highly important that the Tables of Chords and Cadences in this book be written out in full.   This gives the student practice in writing in all keys and assures that all chords have been covered.

After the book has been finished, the pupil should be required to write out the Tables without the aid of Key Signatures. The value of this is obvious.

Ear Training

It is, perhaps, unnecessary to point out that all Chords should be recognized *by their sound* as well as *by their appearance* on the printed page.

Pupils should be encouraged to play all written examples on the keyboard, over and over, thus training the Ear as well as the Eye in recognition of chords and intervals.

At each lesson the teacher should give Ear Drills until the various chords can be distinguished the moment they are heard.

Perhaps a warning against progressing too fast will not be amiss.   Each step in Chord building leads into the next step and new lessons should not be assigned until each exercise is thoroughly mastered by Sight and by Sound.

J. T.

It is assumed that the pupil has studied John Thompson's SCALE-SPELLER (in which Intervals are treated) before beginning this book.

Since all chords are built in *"Third-Steps"* it is advisable to preface the work with a review of Major and Minor Thirds.

MAJOR AND MINOR THIRDS

A MAJOR THIRD is separated by the distance of *4 half-steps.*

A MINOR THIRD is smaller and separated by *3 half-steps.*

Example:

Major Third

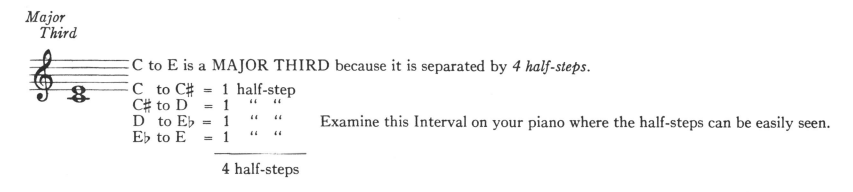

C to E is a MAJOR THIRD because it is separated by *4 half-steps.*

C to C# = 1 half-step
C# to D = 1 " "
D to E♭ = 1 " "   Examine this Interval on your piano where the half-steps can be easily seen.
E♭ to E = 1 " "
———————————
4 half-steps

Minor Third

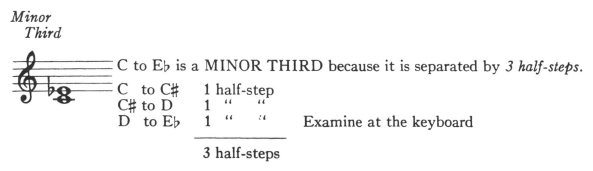

C to E♭ is a MINOR THIRD because it is separated by *3 half-steps.*

C to C#   1 half-step
C# to D   1 "   "
D to E♭   1 "   "   Examine at the keyboard
———————————
3 half-steps

Minor Third

C# to E is a MINOR THIRD—Count the half-steps on the piano keyboard.

W.M.Co. 6535

EXERCISES IN MAJOR AND MINOR THIRDS

Mark Major Thirds—Maj.

Mark Minor Thirds—min.

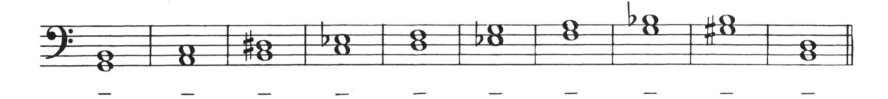

Fill in the *upper* notes to complete the following THIRDS.

Add accidentals (sharps or flats) as necessary.   COUNT THE HALF-STEPS.

IMPORTANT—It is very necessary to recognize Major and Minor Thirds by ear as well as by sight.   Play them on your piano many times until you can hear the difference the moment they are sounded.

W.M.Co. 6535

CHORDS

A CHORD is a group of three or more related tones.

ROOT

The ROOT is the note upon which the chord is built.

All chords are built by adding THIRDS (one above the other) to the Root.

Every chord is NAMED FOR ITS ROOT.

TRIADS

A TRIAD is a chord of THREE tones and consists of a ROOT with its THIRD and FIFTH.

BUILDING TRIADS

To build a Triad on C, we take C as the Root, E as the 3rd, and G as the 5th.

C as Root

With E as 3rd

and G as 5th

Using the following notes as Roots, build Triads by adding the Third and Fifth.

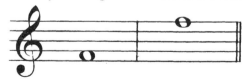

BROKEN CHORDS

When the notes of a chord are sounded together thus, — — they produce the usual chord effect.

When separated, they form what is known as a BROKEN CHORD. For example:

There are many forms of the BROKEN CHORD—sometimes used as Melody, sometimes as accompaniment.

Mark the Root, 3rd and 5th in the following Broken-chord figures.

W.M.Co. 6535

CHORD FIGURES

USED AS MELODY AND ACCOMPANIMENT

In the following examples both the Melody and Accompaniment are formed by Chord Figures.

Fill in the left-hand accompaniments by repeating the chord-pattern shown in the first measure of each example. First write them, then play them on your piano.

MAJOR AND MINOR TRIADS

Triads, like Intervals exist in various forms.

A MAJOR TRIAD is one having a *Major Third* and *Perfect Fifth* (always counting upward from the Root.)

A MINOR TRIAD has a *Minor Third* and a *Perfect Fifth*.

Example

C Major Triad

C to G is a Perfect 5th.

C to E is a *Major* 3rd.

C Minor Triad

C to G is a Perfect 5th.

C to E♭ is a *Minor* 3rd

Change the following Major Triads into Minor Triads.

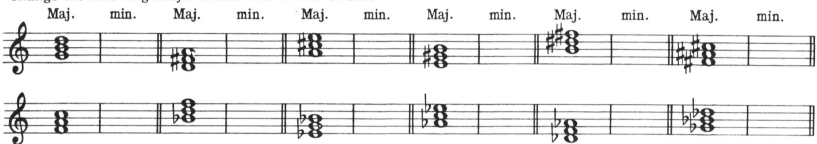

Change the following Minor Triads into Major Triads.

W.M.Co. 6535

THE DIMINISHED TRIAD

A DIMINISHED TRIAD is one having a *Minor Third* and *Diminished Fifth*.
It is therefore *smaller* than the Minor Triad.

Diminished Triad
on C

C to G♭ is a Diminished Fifth.

C to E♭ is a Minor Third.

Two Minor Thirds above each other.

Compare the following Triads and note how each one becomes smaller as the intervals are lowered.

Major Triad on C

Major Third
Perfect Fifth

Minor Triad on C

Minor Third
Perfect Fifth
(3rd has been lowered)

Diminished Triad on C

Minor Third
Diminished Fifth
(3rd and 5th have been lowered)

The Diminished Triad is easily recognized as it is the only Triad with two minor thirds above each other (counting upward from the Root).

Change the following Minor Triads into Diminished Triads (by lowering the fifth).

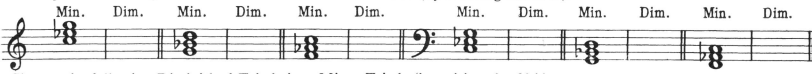

Change the following Diminished Triads into Minor Triads (by raising the fifth).

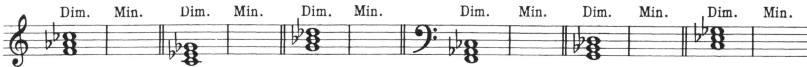

Mark the Triads below as follows: min. = Minor; Dim. = Diminished.
Be sure to compute the Thirds in each Triad, remembering that the Diminished Triad is the only one with two minor thirds.

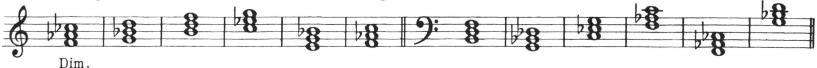

W.M.Co. 6535

THE AUGMENTED TRIAD

The AUGMENTED TRIAD has a Major Third and an AUGMENTED Fifth.
It is therefore *bigger* than the Major Triad.

Major Triad on C   Augmented Triad on C

Two Major Thirds above each other.

C to G♯ is an Augmented Fifth.
C to E is a Major Third.

The Augmented Triad can be recognized from the fact that it is the only Triad with two major thirds above each other (counting upward from the Root).

Change the following Major Triads into Augmented Triads (by raising the fifth).

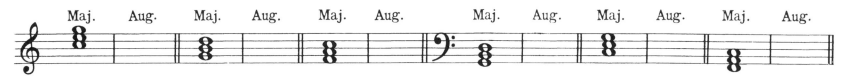

Change the following Augmented Triads into Major Triads (by lowering the fifth).

Mark the Triads below as follows:
Maj. = Major
min. = Minor
Dim. = Diminished
Aug. = Augmented

Play the above Triads many times over on your piano until you can recognize them by their sound.

W.M.Co. 6535

WRITING EXERCISES

Write the four forms of the Triad (Major, Minor, Diminished and Augmented) on the Roots below.

Be careful of the spelling.   Use what Accidentals are necessary but *never* change the letter-names of the 1st, 3rd and 5th of the Triad.

In building the Triads be sure to measure the size of each Third contained in the chord.

TABLE OF TRIADS
ON ALL DEGREES OF THE MAJOR SCALE

Triads can be built on any degree of the scale, as shown in the Table below.

Note that Triads on the 1st., 4th., and 5th. degrees of the Major Scale are MAJOR TRIADS.

The Triads on the 2nd., 3rd., and 6th. degrees are MINOR TRIADS.

The Triad on the 7th. degree is a DIMINISHED TRIAD.

Fill up the following Table by writing Triads on each degree of the scale.

TABLE OF TRIADS
(continued)

MAJOR I	minor 2	minor 3	MAJOR IV	MAJOR V	minor 6	diminished 7

After writing the Triads on this and the preceding page, play them on your piano.

Listen intently so that you can learn to distinguish *by ear*, the difference between Major, Minor and Diminished Triads.

TEACHERS' NOTE—Later on, as pupils become more familiar with Triads in various Keys, they should be required to fill out a Table like the one above *except that it should have no Key Signatures*, thus compelling the pupil to place the proper Accidentals where they belong.

Space will be found at the end of the book for this and other additional exercises.

INVERSION means that a chord has been *changed* from its Root Position.

When the Root is *not* on the bottom the chord is INVERTED.

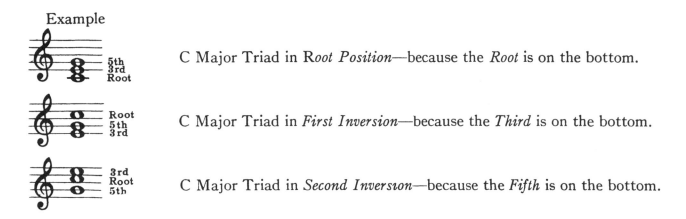

C Major Triad in *Root Position*—because the *Root* is on the bottom.

C Major Triad in *First Inversion*—because the *Third* is on the bottom.

C Major Triad in *Second Inversion*—because the *Fifth* is on the bottom.

PLAY THE FOLLOWING TRIADS ON YOUR PIANO

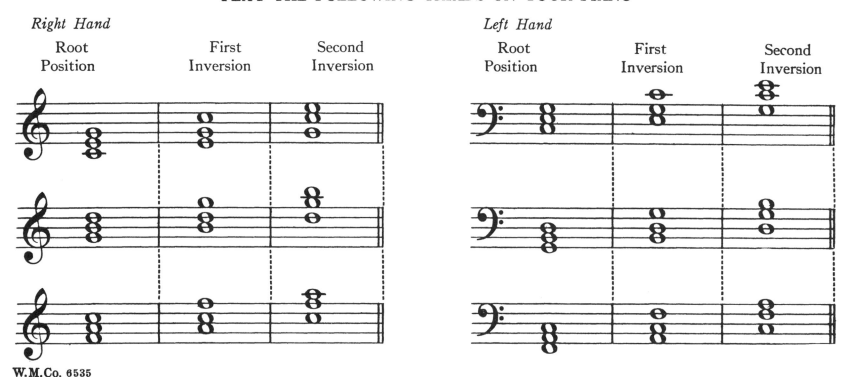

HOW TO KNOW WHEN A CHORD IS INVERTED
(BY USE OF THE PATTERN-OF-THIRDS)

Here is the way to recognize an Inverted chord.

All chords are built in THIRD-STEPS, therefore,

When all the notes of a chord are evenly spaced—A THIRD APART—the chord is in ROOT POSITION.

When the notes of a chord are NOT evenly spaced in Thirds, the chord is INVERTED.

RECOGNIZING THE ROOT

THE ROOT IS ALWAYS THE FIRST NOTE (counting upward) TO BREAK THE ORDER OF THIRDS.

Root
Position

 E to G is a 3rd

C to E is a 3rd   Perfect order of THIRDS—Therefore in ROOT POSITION—C is the Root.

1st
Inversion

 G TO C IS A FOURTH

E to G is a 3rd   The order of THIRDS is broken showing chord has been INVERTED.

C is the Root because it causes the interval of a FOURTH in the Chord.

2nd
Inversion

 C to E is a 3rd

G TO C IS A FOURTH

Again the order of THIRDS is broken.   Chord is therefore INVERTED.

C is again the Root because it creates a FOURTH.

W.M.Co. 6535

EXERCISES IN FINDING THE ROOT

By use of the Rule just learned, find and write the letter-name of the Root in each of the following Chords.   Mark the position of each chord thus: R = Root Position

                         1 = 1st Inversion

                         2 = 2nd Inversion

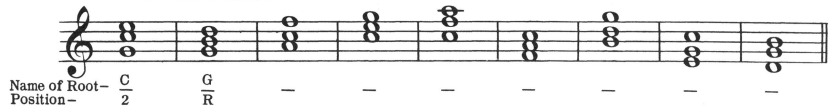

Name of Root— $\dfrac{C}{2}$ $\dfrac{G}{R}$ —   —   —   —   —   —   —
Position—

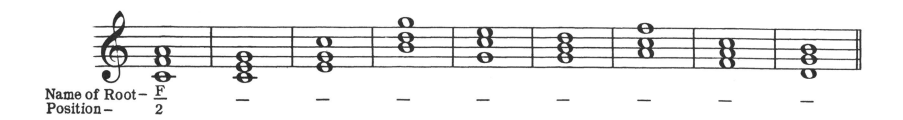

Name of Root— $\dfrac{C}{R}$ —   —   —   —   —   —   —   —
Position—

Name of Root— $\dfrac{F}{2}$ —   —   —   —   —   —   —   —
Position—

Name of Root— $\dfrac{G}{2}$ —   —   —   —   —   —   —   —
Position—

W.M.Co. 6535

WRITING INVERTED TRIADS

Write Major Triads in the positions indicated.   R = Root Position—1 = 1st Inversion—2 = 2nd Inversion.

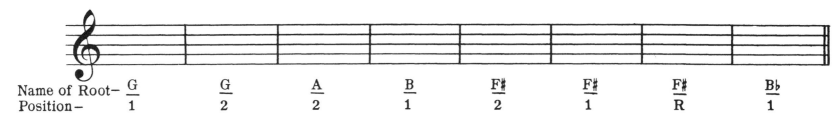

Name of Root—	G	G	A	B	F♯	F♯	F♯	B♭
Position—	1	2	2	1	2	1	R	1

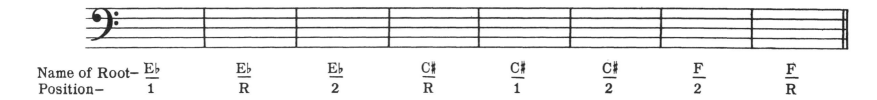

Name of Root—	E♭	E♭	E♭	C♯	C♯	C♯	F	F
Position—	1	R	2	R	1	2	2	R

Write Minor Triads in the positions called for below.

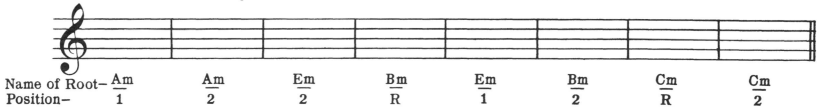

Name of Root—	Am	Am	Em	Bm	Em	Bm	Cm	Cm
Position—	1	2	2	R	1	2	R	2

Name of Root—	Fm	Fm	Fm	Dm	Dm	Dm	B♭m	B♭m
Position—	2	1	R	R	1	2	2	1

W.M.Co. 6535

The Table of Triads on page 12 shows that every Major Scale has THREE MAJOR TRIADS.
They are found on the FIRST, FOURTH and FIFTH degrees of the Scale.

The Triad on the 1st degree is called the TONIC TRIAD.
The Triad on the 5th degree is called the DOMINANT TRIAD.
The Triad on the 4th degree is called the SUB-DOMINANT TRIAD.

These THREE MAJOR TRIADS are very important.
First, they are closely related to each other.
Secondly, they have a particular significance, which will be learned later.

Let us first examine their RELATION.

CHORD RELATION

Chords are related just like people.
In your own house for instance, you may be a son or a daughter.
But when you are in your uncle's house you become a nephew or niece.
You are *the same person* in each case—but your RELATION has changed.

See how the C MAJOR TRIAD changes its relation as it moves from one house to another (one key to another).

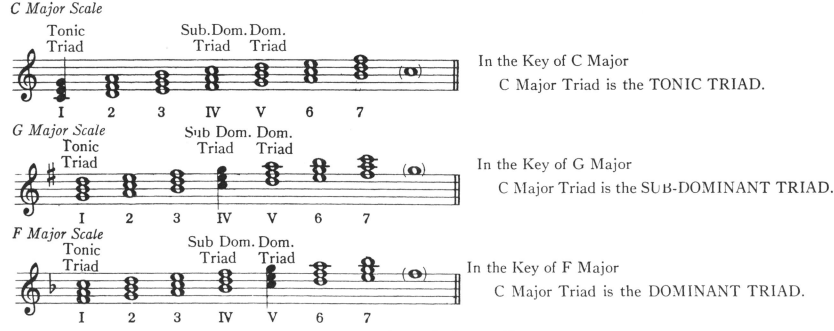

The chord remains the same—but changes its RELATION as it changes Key.
The other Major Triads of course, change their relation in a similar manner.

CHORD RELATION

Mark the relation of the following chords by writing

I   for TONIC Triads
IV   for SUB-DOMINANT Triads
and
V   for DOMINANT Triads

In C Major

In G Major

In F Major

PROGRESSION OF CHORDS

(Tonic to Dominant)

In the early days—before instruments were made—all music was sung.

It would thus require three voices to sing the tones of a Triad together as a chord.

To-day, even in instrumental music, we still refer to the different tones of a chord as "voices"

When one chord progresses to another it is always desirable to have the "voices" move as smoothly as possible.
There are two simple rules that bring this about.

Rule 1—If the same tone belongs to both chords, KEEP IT IN THE SAME VOICE.

Rule 2—Move each of the other voices TO THE NEAREST TONE in the new chord.

For example: Suppose we are in the Key of C Major and want to move from the TONIC chord to the DOMINANT chord.

It will be seen from the above example that in passing from the TONIC TRIAD to the DOMINANT TRIAD one tone (the 5th) remains stationary and each of the other voices move *downward* to the nearest tone of the following Triad, which happens to be the next degree (downward) of the Scale.

To return to the TONIC TRIAD the process is simply reversed thus:

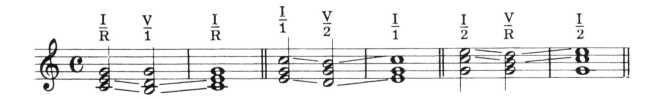

HARMONIZING MELODIES—By use of Tonic and Dominant chords

Harmonize the following examples as directed—Be sure to move the voices as smoothly as possible.
When any tone in one chord belongs also in the next chord, *keep it in the same voice.*

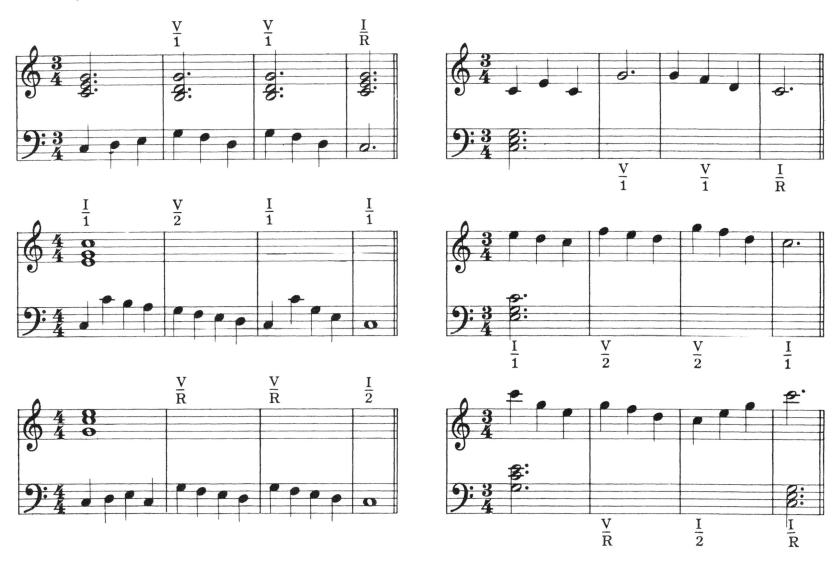

PROGRESSION OF CHORDS

(Tonic to Sub-Dominant)

In progressing from the TONIC TRIAD to the SUB-DOMINANT TRIAD, one tone (the Root) remains stationary and the other two voices move *upward* to the next degree of the Scale.

Tonic to Sub-Dominant   Tonic to Sub-Dominant to Tonic

HARMONIZING MELODIES

By use of the TONIC and SUB-DOMINANT TRIADS

Add the Harmonies to the following Melodies—remembering to *keep one tone stationary* and to move the other voices *to the nearest tone* (one degree up or down) in the following chord.

THE CADENCE

A CADENCE is the end (or Close) of a musical progression.

In simple music you will usually find one at the end of every fourth measure.

There are many varieties of CADENCES but for the present we shall study only the more usual ones.

The THREE MAJOR TRIADS play an important role in forming CADENCES.

An AUTHENTIC CADENCE is one in which the last two chords form a progression from V to I.

A PLAGAL CADENCE is formed when the last two chords progress from IV to I.

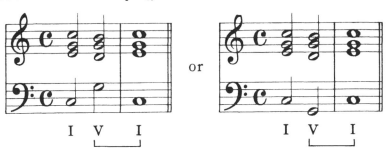 or

AUTHENTIC AND PLAGAL CADENCES

In the following examples mark Authentic Cadences with *A* and Plagal Cadences with *P*.

THE FULL AUTHENTIC CADENCE
(Sometimes called COMPOUND CADENCE)

The FULL AUTHENTIC CADENCE includes all three of the MAJOR TRIADS and is formed as follows:

I, IV, I, V, I.   All Triads are in Root Position except the Tonic Triad when it appears *between IV and V* in which instance t is in the Second Inversion.

Example
In C Major

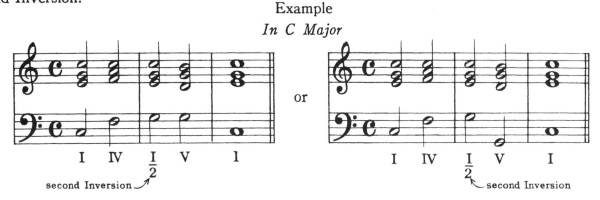

TABLE OF FULL AUTHENTIC CADENCES
in all Major Keys

Fill in the following Table of Full Authentic Cadences.

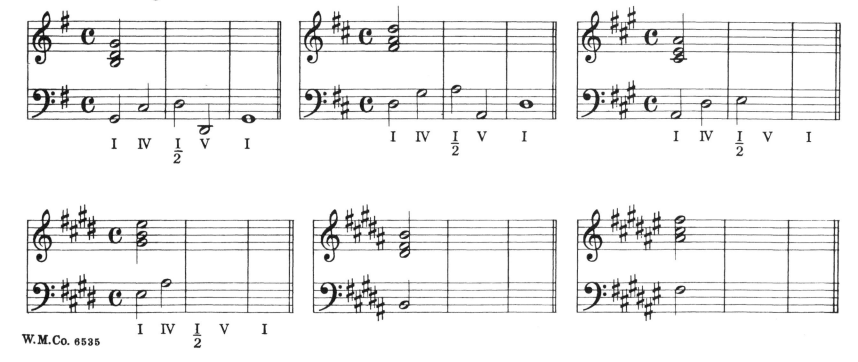

TABLE OF FULL AUTHENTIC CADENCES
(continued)

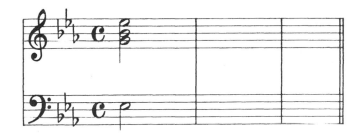
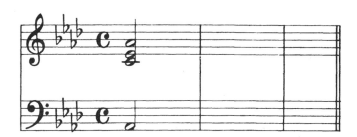

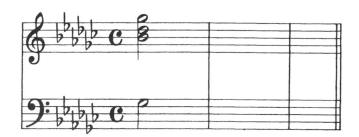

W.M.Co. 6535

THE DOMINANT SEVENTH CHORD

The DOMINANT SEVENTH CHORD is formed simply by adding a minor third to the Major Triad found on the Dominant.

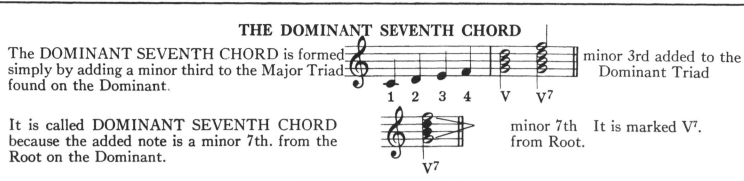

minor 3rd added to the Dominant Triad

It is called DOMINANT SEVENTH CHORD because the added note is a minor 7th. from the Root on the Dominant.

minor 7th from Root. It is marked V⁷.

THREE INVERSIONS

Since it is a four-note chord it can appear in four Positions—Root Position and three Inversions.

| Root Position | 1st Inversion | 2nd Inversion | 3rd Inversion |

PROGRESSION TO THE TONIC

The Dominant Seventh Chord usually progresses to the Tonic Chord and may be used in Cadences.

Example

The 5th. and 7th. move *down* to the next degree of the scale.
The 3rd. moves *up* to the next degree of the scale.
The Root remains stationary.

Complete the following progressions (from Dom. 7th to Tonic) moving the voices as shown above.

THE DIMINISHED SEVENTH CHORD

The DIMINISHED SEVENTH CHORD is formed by adding a minor third to the Diminished Triad found on the 7th. degree of the Scale.

1 2 3 4 5 6 7

minor 3rd added to the Diminished Triad.

It is called DIMINISHED SEVENTH CHORD because the added note is a Diminished 7th. from the Root.

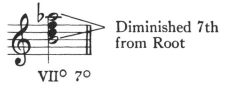

Diminished 7th from Root

VII° 7°

THREE INVERSIONS

Like the Dominant Seventh Chord the Diminished Seventh Chord has four Positions—Root Position and 3 Inversions.

Root Position   1st Inversion   2nd Inversion   3rd Inversion

PROGRESSION TO THE TONIC

The Diminished Seventh Chord progresses to the Tonic Chord as follows.

7th. descends
5th. descends
3rd. ascends
Root ascends

Complete the following progressions (from Dim. 7th. chord to Tonic) moving the voices as shown above.

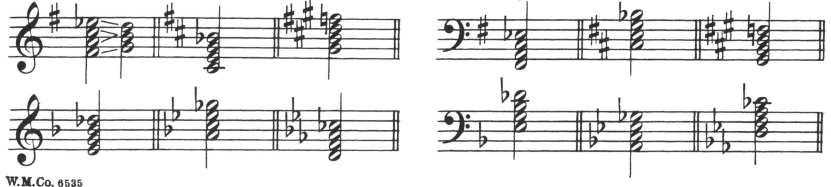

TABLE OF
Dominant and Diminished 7th Chords, progressing to the Tonic

Complete the following Table of Dom. and Dim. 7th chords.
Be careful to add the proper Accidental to the top note of the Diminished 7th chord.

TABLE OF TRIADS
on *Harmonic Minor Scales*

Fill in the following Table.

Do not forget to raise the 7th degree of the Scale each time it appears in a Triad.

TABLE OF TRIADS
on Harmonic Minor Scales
(continued)

minor 1	*diminished* 2	Augmented 3	minor 4	MAJOR V	MAJOR VI	*diminished* 7

W.M.Co. 6535